IMAGES OF ENGLAND

RAMSGATE AND ST LAWRENCE REVISITED

IMAGES OF ENGLAND

RAMSGATE AND ST LAWRENCE REVISITED

DON DIMOND

TEMPUS

Frontispiece: Kent Terrace, as viewed from the harbour yard. Chalk was excavated in 1833-37 and the terrace was built behind the bazaar, which included a large restaurant owned by Mr Vassalli which was later owned by Mr Luigi Gatti & Sons. He eventually sold most of the property to the Marzetti family but kept a section which he opened as a pub called the Prince of Wales, *c.* 1885. The licensing Justices closed it in 1909. Note the bare white cliffs to the right of the terrace, not to be seen today.

First published 2006

Tempus Publishing Limited
The Mill, Brimscombe Port,
Stroud, Gloucestershire, GL5 2QG
www.tempus-publishing.com

British Library Cataloguing in Publication Data.
A catalogue record for this book is available from the British Library.

ISBN 0 7524 3868 9

Typesetting and origination by Tempus Publishing Limited.
Printed in Great Britain.

Contents

Acknowledgements

Bob Bradley and staff at Margate Old Town Hall and Local History Museum; Michael Hunt and staff at Ramsgate Maritime Museum; Mr and Mrs Peter Chisholm; Mrs Joyce Burlinson; Mr George Matthews; Mr Barrie Wootton; Mr Ross Palmer; Mr John William; and Sandi Dimond, who typed this manuscript.

Sources

Cotton's *History and Antiquities of the Church and Parish of St Lawrence.*
C.F. Dendy Marshall, *A History of the Southern Railways.*
Derrick Molock, *The Life and Times of the East Kent Critic.*
East Kent Times.
F.J. Parsons, *Ramsgate Illustrated.*
J. Huddleston, *400 Facts and Curiosities of Ramsgate.*
John Lewis, *The History and Antiquities of the Isle of Thanet.*
Kelly's *Directory of the Isle of Thanet.*
Lewis Hepworth, *Twenty Pictures of Ramsgate.*
S.E. Winbolt, *Kent-Bell's Pocket Guide.*
St Lawrence in Thanet, Nine Hundred Years.
St Lawrence Old and New.
The Borough Pocket Guide to Ramsgate.
Thanet's *Raid History.*

Introduction

Ramsgate is a special place. The richness of its architecture, the beauty of its coastline and the area's unique place in history all contribute to making Ramsgate special. But are these features what genuinely make the town different?

It is true that Ramsgate does have unique buildings and street scapes. Where else would you find Regency façades designed to be viewed as you approach from the sea or a parish church that stands so proudly above the town? Also, without doubt, the wonderful Royal Harbour is unrivalled anywhere else in the world. No wonder Pugin, one of the greatest architects the world has known, made Ramsgate his home.

The ever-changing skies that inspired Turner, the coastline from Pegwell Bay through Dumpton Gap to Ramsgate, with its salt marshes, orchids and rich bird life, its smooth golden sands and crumbling chalk cliffs, all contribute to making Ramsgate special.

Few places surpass Ramsgate and the area around it for historical significance. Julius Caesar invaded Britain through Pegwell Bay and conquered the land from his base at Richborough. Legend has it that Hengest and Horsa also landed in the bay, making it the birthplace of England. St Augustine also came ashore here, bringing Christianity with him. If he had only built his church where he landed instead of inland at Canterbury, today the Archbishop of Ramsgate would be the head of the Church of England!

But these are not the things that make Ramsgate special to me. What makes Ramsgate special to me is its human scale. Nothing is too big and nothing is over the top in the town, and the memory of each passing generation builds into its fabric. It is a town built for ordinary people which for centuries has inspired them to do extraordinary things.

Much of the town was built to fight Napoleon and as you walk around the Harbour and through the streets it is easy to imagine the bustle of preparations for war. In my mind's eye it is not the generals and the admirals that I can see in Ramsgate's roads but the enlisted men, the gunners and the troopers pulling their carts and loading the ships or drinking in the taverns and parading in the squares.

Ramsgate is a town where people have lived for hundreds of years, where they have worked and played through good times and bad, fought and feared, celebrated victory and faced the challenges of defeat. Through it all they have brought up their children, fed their families and got on with their lives.

It is this that the buildings and the streets reflect. They show hundreds of years of English people getting on, doing what is needed, and in the process, without realising they were doing it, leaving their mark and making England great.

I hope that from the pages and pictures that follow you will come to see Ramsgate as I see it. Don Dimond's books are never just about the buildings of the town, they are about the people of the town and what they have made of the special place they inhabit. From these pictures of people at leisure and earning their living, and pictures of all the places where people have done these things over the generations before us, I have no doubt you will get the real flavour of Ramsgate, a truly special place that has produced truly special people.

Stephen Ladyman
Member of Parliament for South Thanet
December 2005

This book is dedicated to the memory of the author's late colleague Mr Kenneth Terry (above) who left us suddenly on 10 December 2001. Ken was an ardent collector of postcards for many years and his subject matter was vast. Prior to retiring, Ken worked for many years for R.R. Rowlands, confectioner, of Harbour Street. I am sure many of you will remember seeing him through the shop window, rolling the popular Ramsgate Rock into shape. He was a pleasant, inoffensive person as all who know him will surely vouch. All royalties from this publication will be donated equally between two charities: The British Heart Foundation and The Fire Service National Benevolent Fund.

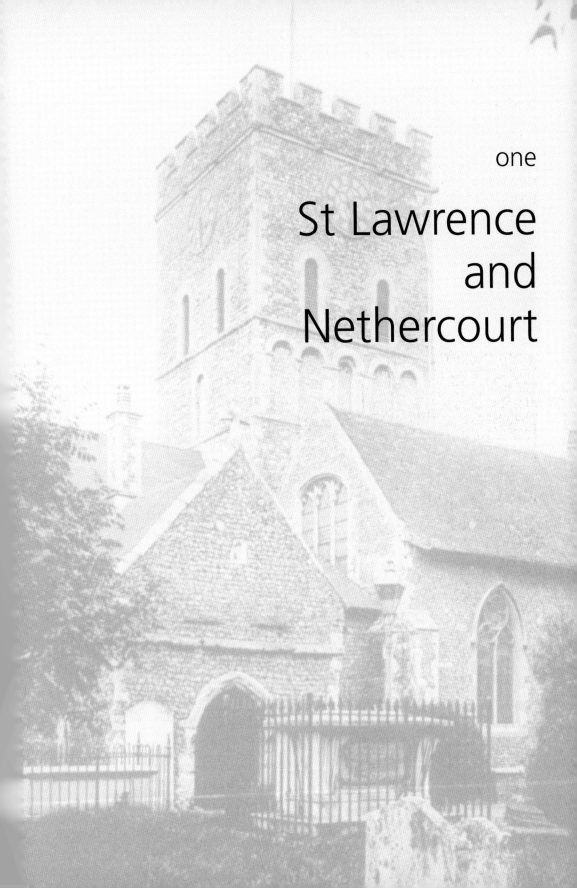

one

St Lawrence
and
Nethercourt

Left: Today, St Lawrence church is still the centrepiece of the village. Many changes have taken place to the building since Saxon times; restoration and enlargement were necessary due to the increase in inhabitants of the village. The churchyard was first consecrated in 1275 and has been enlarged four times. It has also been reduced in size three times, first in 1794, to widen Newington Road, then in 1803, to widen the High Street and finally in 1961, to make Newington Road suitable for modern traffic.

Below: A slightly later view of St Lawrence a very tranquil scene. The Church, being the most dominating organisation, was followed by the people of wealth, like the Weigall family of Southwood House who knew and cared for the well-being of those less fortunate than themselves.

On the Corner of Chapel Road, High Street, St Lawrence Grandpa William Grimley Lawrence stands proudly outside his bakery shop. The 'Hearty Congratulations' banner could be alluding to the 1902 Coronation of King Edward VII and Queen Alexandra. Sadly, all of these buildings were demolished for the road widening of St Lawrence High Street.

This view of St Lawrence High Street in 1920 illustrates the density of the buildings in the village. In the centre of the view can be seen the Wheatsheaf Inn, on the left is the Rose Inn, followed by the St Lawrence parish hall, the Fire Escape Station and St Lawrence post office. On the right in the far distance is the White Horse Inn; John Churchill, boot maker; and John Jarman, blacksmith; Mary Miller, dressmaker; and George Philpott, butcher, making up a close-knit business community at this time.

This postcard of Nethercourt in 1917 was sent to a Miss Humphrey in Ireland during the time that Nethercourt was being used as an auxiliary hospital. Note the view of the Lodge in the lower left-hand corner.

This is a view of the Toll House in Nethercourt. In the background can be seen the narrow road to Canterbury with wide, open fields beyond. The pony and trap, with an unknown gentleman, depicts a more laid-back mode of transport. The Toll House was eventually demolished to make way for the new London Road improvements.

St Lawrence High Street, *c.* 1925. Following a demolition order in 1938, some sixty-one properties that lined the west, or right-hand, side of this view were demolished for road widening, thus trebling the width of the road into Ramsgate. Strangely, today we are seeing the reverse of these decisions. Traffic islands and lay-bys for parking vehicles are once again restricting the width of the roads.

The heart of the village of St Lawrence, 1951. To the left we can see the Rose Inn and next door on the right is J.C. Morrison Ltd, motor car agents and engineers. The centrepiece is St Lawrence church on the corner of Newington Road. Across the road is the White Horse public house. Sadly, both the Rose Inn and the White Horse have long gone. Finally, on the right is the Wheatsheaf Inn which at the time of writing was up for sale.

Manston Road in St Lawrence, c. 1926. The building immediately on the right is called Manston Cottage. It was, at one time, a florist and nursery owned by Richard May & Son but was later to be occupied by a Mrs E. Daniels. Latterly, the grounds were incorporated into the St Lawrence Laundry complex. Today the area contains a small industrial estate.

On the right-hand side of this view of Manston Road, c. 1925, can be seen the old St Lawrence vicarage which was demolished in the early 1960s. On the opposite side are the Bay View Villas and the entrance to Clifton Road.

Manston Road level crossing and the gatehouse, *c.* 1924. Alfred Morris was the railway gatekeeper. Soon after this photograph major changes were to take place, including the building of a road bridge which made life easier for one and all.

Manston Court Road, at some point between 1948-59. This fine horse and carriage, belonging to Manston Court Dairies' proprietor Mr C.N. Austen, was entered in a competition of four-wheeled horse-drawn commercial vehicles. Unfortunately there is no record of any prize.

Newington Road, St Margaret's, *c.* 1936. This property is very near the junction of Holbrook Drive and St James Avenue and the houses you see in the bottom left are part of the Whitehall estate. The construction of this part of St James Avenue is yet to take place. This view was taken by local photographers Carr & Son.

Saverite, Newington Road, 1974. This grocery shop on the corner of Queen's Avenue has seen a few changes over the years. For nearly two decades this shop was occupied by H. Wood & Co., grocers and butchers, until 1969 when it was taken over by Saverite, the proprietors being a couple who came from South Africa. The next change came in the mid-1980s when it became First Stop but once again the inevitable happened and its latest name is Best Moon Shop: a grocery store, off-licence, newsagents and video rental shop.

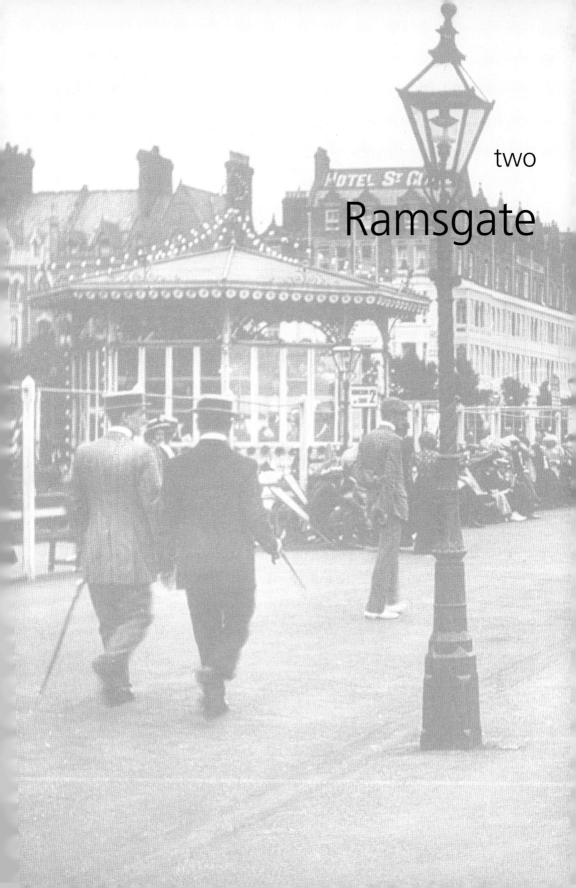

two

Ramsgate

Left: This is Mount Zion Chapel on Camden Road (previously called Clover Hill). It was erected in 1843 and is of gothic design, with brick and stone dressings and intersecting tracery. A strict Baptist church and Sunday school, it was demolished in the 1970s.

Below: Ramsgate High Street, *c.* 1830, looking from Hardres Street and taken well before the Amphitheatre, which was built in 1883, came about. Over the years there have been many changes to this site. The Amphitheatre became the new Palace Theatre after the building was entirely reconstructed at a cost of £5,000 in 1907/08. It was used as such right up until 1961 but Dye & Son, Furnishers, utilized part of the site in 1963, as did Hardy & Co., furnishers, and Busy B Supermarket in 1967. Fine Fare grocers moved there in 1974 and the Green Shield Stamp gift shop was also located here. The building is currently occupied by Argos.

Chartham Terrace as viewed from the Westcliff Promenade. The architect and builder of this imposing structure was Mr Charles Habershon.

Liverpool Lawn, previously known as Liverpool Terrace, 1924. The properties were built between 1827 and 1836 and were named after Lord Warden of the Cinque Ports and Lord Liverpool, who was a frequent visitor to Ramsgate in the reign of William IV. An apex can be seen at the centre of the buildings; within it lies a crest or armorial insignia, visible but badly worn with age.

Left: Addington Street, *c.* 1912. A detachment of volunteers of the Kent Cyclist Battalion are marching along the street, probably on their way to the annual camp. On the left is the sign of R.J. Yare, hosier, and on the right, the dairy of Fred Wellard Jnr.

Below: Nelson Crescent, 1920, named in honour of Horatio, Viscount Nelson. The crescent was built in 1798, delightfully situated overlooking the Royal Harbour and is one of the most favoured residential parts of the town. This locality was once known as St George's Fields.

The Paragon, 1911, on the junction with Addington Street. This is quite a relaxing view and was taken during the month of August. Note the Addington Street post office, the fish hawkers and the Corporation horse and cart.

Ramsgate public library and Guilford Lawn, c. 1910. This depiction of a winter scene is quite a contrast to what happened on Friday 13 August 2004 when, tragically, disaster struck during the evening and this listed building was engulfed in flames. It was almost completely destroyed by the fire – the building was just two months away from celebrating its centenary. Many treasures were irreplaceably lost. Hopefully, when the new building rises from the ashes, more measures will be taken to ensure that the building and its contents are kept safe.

Looking at this view of Vale Villes, *c.* 1848, it is hard to imagine this as the Vale Square of today. Here we see illustrated the wide open spaces that have now been built on. Also note the bathing machines in the bottom left-hand corner. Designed in the early English style, Christ Church was consecrated in August 1847 by Archbishop Howley.

A lovely group photograph in Vale Square depicting Revd J.H. Askwith parading with some of his Christ Church flock around 1918. He took up his duties in Ramsgate in 1912 and continued his ministry for eighteen years before retiring in 1930.

Another part of our vanished Ramsgate, this is the Congregation Hall, George Street, 1973. The hall was built in 1894 and Sir W.H. Wills Bart laid a memorial stone on 12 March 1894. The entrance to Meeting Street can just be seen at the corner of the hall and if you progressed along you would find an extensive graveyard. This was all removed many years ago to make space for the building of private dwellings.

Left: This impressive building, on Victoria Parade and at the corner of D'este Road, was once the office of the Ministry of Social Services. Though it is now in private ownership, it is still a very elegant-looking property.

Below: Ellington Baptist Chapel, sited on the junction of Duncan Road and Crescent Road, was erected in 1891 for the princely sum of £870. It was demolished in the early 1970s to make way for a superb block of six flats called Bowen Court.

This quaint old cottage on Southwood Road, seen here around 1885, was at one time to be found located on the west side of the road where there now stands a children's pre-school nursery called Stay & Play. The lady just inside the gate is believed to be Mrs E. Philpott.

Southwood Road, 1913. If you were to take a leisurely stroll along this road today you would hardly notice any change but for the lack of trees, which have long since been removed. This is still a very pleasant area in which to reside.

Left: This devastating scene of Flora Road, 24 February 1903, depicts a tragically sad event. A terrible explosion was set off by Samuel Henson after his wife Jane refused conciliation after they had experienced a long period of turbulent misery and constant arguing. The explosion was intended for their lodger but instead it killed Samuel's son, William John Henson and caused extensive injuries to his mother and father.

Below: Flora Road, February 1903. At the close of Samuel Henson's trial, he was found guilty of murder and sentenced to death. Fortunately for him, many of the people who knew him thought that he was mentally ill and petitioned for leniency. They were successful in getting Samuel's sentence reduced from death by hanging to life imprisonment.

This is York Street on the corner of York Terrace showing the tobacconist and Private Bar here before their decline after the Second World War. This part of Ramsgate has now been regenerated. The Isle of Thanet Motor Co. has long gone and today the buildings on this corner are part of the Swallow Kent International hotel group, previously known as the Ramada Jarvis Hotel, of Harbour Parade.

Screaming Alley, Westcliff, got its name as follows: it is reputed that in November 1883 a horse and cart ran away from Grange Road down to the alley and went straight over the cliff. An alternative suggestion is that 'screaming' comes from the ghost a nun who had been walled-up alive for having an affair with one of the monks who lived in the abbey (on the right in the view). Sometime later, during the Second World War, a soldier on guard duty on the cliffs had gone missing and was eventually found in a terrible state. His hair had turned white and all he could say was, 'She was in white and she came through the wall towards me waving her outstretched hands, as if pleading for help'. Sadly, after this terrifying experience he was invalided out of the army!

Left: Albion Place, 6 June 1915. This postcard to Mademoiselle Maynaud of Paris was sent by the daughter, Clara Hitchcock, of this well-established boarding house, Rock View, thanking her for her kind thoughts towards them following the raids and bombing of the town.

Below: Little is required to be said about this card featuring Effingham Street. Arthur Larkin served as mayor to Ramsgate from 1921-22, was a member of the Education Committee and was Chairman of Governors at Chatham House County School when it opened in 1909. Eventually he rose to the Aldermanic Bench. He retired from the council in 1915 after twenty-one years of service.

Arthur Larkin & Co · 16 · Arthur Larkin & Co

AGT

SANITARY SPECIALISTS.

14 & 16 Effingham Street, RAMSGATE.

TELEPHONE 11Y.   ESTABLISHED 1836.

The Best House in THANET

FOR

Decorative Work

In connection with

RESIDENCES, CHURCHES and PUBLIC BUILDINGS.

Structural Alterations and Up=to=date Sanitation.

For over a quarter of a century Leonard Spratling prospered with his drapery and haberdashery business, depicted here at No. 113 King Street, on the corner of Alma Place. The prices of the items on display are quite entertaining; the most expensive item being 2s 6d. The property today has been completely changed and is now a very pleasant private dwelling.

Leonard Spratling, resplendent in his Masonic regalia, c. 1900. He belonged to the Royal Navy Lodge, No. 429. Meetings were held on the first day of each month at the Royal Hotel, Harbour Street, the proprietor being J.J. Roach.

Left: This view of Harbour Street, in 1904, was taken prior to the visit of HRH Princess Louise to the town on 29 June. Nearly every building was dressed out with flags and bunting, thus decorating the area and ensuring a grand impression was made on the princess. As can be seen, it was a very successful effort by the townsfolk.

Below: The market place, 1904. These magnificent decorations, surmounted by a crown, link the four main streets of Ramsgate and were an ideal canopy for the princess to travel under. To the left is the Town Hall, and at the beginning of Queen Street is the shop belonging to J. Mathew, watchmaker. Looking up the High Street, on the right, is G. & T. Rowe, ironmongers.

Albion Place and Gardens, constructed between 1789-91. These properties fast became fashionable residences for the well-off people of Ramsgate. To the left in the view we can just see the entrance to Abbott's Hill. Destiny, the beautiful and striking piece of work by sculptor Mr Gilbert Bays, can be seen in *Ramsgate and St Lawrence*, on p. 35.

The statue Destiny, though sadly not in this view of Albion Place and Gardens, was refurbished and unveiled at 3.15 p.m. on Friday 17 December 2004. Thanet Council carried out the work, with donations being made by local groups including the Ramsgate Society.

The Truro Court Hotel, East Cliff was previously the Casa Blanca Hotel. The new owners, Improved Hotels Ltd, acquired the residency and grounds known as Chylton Lodge, No. 33 Augusta Road. The acquisition of the two properties, with the merging of the grounds including putting greens and tennis courts, has given the company a site in a splendid position facing the sea and harbour. With accommodation for sixty guests, it is also close to the marina pool and has access to the amusements just below the cliff. After a complete restoration the hotel opened on 29 May 1936.

The cluster of trees makes this scene of Truro Court Hotel, viewed from the eastern side, very pleasing to the eye. Sadly over the years, with the decline of the holiday trade, the hotel was closed and the property demolished. The area stood vacant for some years but eventually a fine new building took its place and today it is known as Home Fleet House for private residents. The hotel used this postcard as a promotional item.

Elegantly dressed people taking a leisurely stroll along Victoria Parade on the East Cliff. The prominent building, is of course, the Hotel St Cloud, later to be renamed the San Clu. Today it has a new name as the business has been taken over by the Comfort Inn hotel chain.

A pristine group of staff employed by the Hotel St Cloud, on Victoria Parade. Unfortunately the names are unknown. Note the name of the hotel, however, on the collars of some of the staff, who are all very smartly attired.

HM Coastguard Station, Victoria Parade, *c.* 1920. This station replaced the previous one which was sited, close to the Augusta Steps, on land required for the new Sands railway station, originally built in 1865. Modernisation and cost-cutting soon made these premises obsolete and they were finally closed down in 1955 and converted for housing by the Ramsgate Corporation.

Ramsgate cemetery and Memorial Chapel, Cecilia Road. Previously known as Cemetery Road, the chapel is open daily to the public from 8.00 a.m. to dusk. It is quite an imposing chapel, built of whole flints with stone buttresses by architect George Gilbert Scott, who was largely responsible for the mid-nineteenth century gothic revival in England. The first burial in this cemetery took place in 1871.

three

Harbour
and
Sands

PROVIDER

The above picture, clearly depicting a terrible storm in which the lifeboat *Bradford 3* and the harbour tug *Vulcan* have gone to the assistance of a vessel in trouble, is by Joseph Byrne of Ramsgate and dates from around 1885. The bravery of such men can never be underestimated and this composition was probably inspired by the rescue of a number of crew from the stricken vessel *Indian Chief* on Wednesday 5 January 1881.

Tom Read and Joe Read – two stalwarts of the Ramsgate lifeboat – at Ramsgate harbour. Both were members of the lifeboat crew for nearly fifty years. Joe held the gold medal, presented by the American government, for his assistance in the rescue of twelve of the crew of the American steamship *Piave* of New Jersey, which ran aground on Goodwin Sands in 1919. His brother Tom retired from the position of coxswain of the *Prudential* in September 1935. At one time there were five members of the family serving in the lifeboat crew together. They were brothers Tom, Joe and Will, son Walter and nephew Tom.

A splendid view of the harbour with the regatta in full swing, *c.* 1890. These events would generally take place at the latter end of August each year. Here the inner harbour is surrounded by thousands of spectators witnessing the competitive events which finally culminated in a grand firework display. This photograph is by H.D. Hogben.

Ramsgate harbour regatta and Peace Day celebrations, 1919. After four years of war this occasion was just the tonic the town's people required to lift their spirits. In the middle distance can be seen the cross wall, which retains the water in the inner basin of the harbour, thronged with happy chattering groups of people whose numbers were continually swelled by additions from every part of the town. As usual, numerous events took place. The two vessels (whose names are unknown) bedecked with bunting may be part of a fleet of boarding craft used during the war.

LANDING FISH AT. RAMSGATE.

This view, published by Ramsgate photographer L.G. Carpenter, clearly shows the commercial value of the harbour at this particular period of time – August 1906. At one time there were over 180 registered craft using the harbour. Nearly a century has passed since then and the harbour today is now graced mainly with motor and sailing yachts.

HOME.FOR.XMAS.1906

'Home for Christmas', 1906. The inner basin of the harbour is saturated to capacity with fishing smacks. It is so easy to imagine the fishermen enjoying a well-earned festive break with their families while their apprentices were being entertained at the Ramsgate Home for Smack-Boy's in the harbour. To the left can be seen a section of the new road which was commenced in 1893.

Ramsgate regatta, Thursday 11 August 1910. It is recorded that 10,000 spectators attended this event at the inner harbour. Here we have just a small section of them as they enjoy a front-seat view. The parliamentary member for Thanet, Norman Craig, was in the committee enclosure and the Mayoress of Ramsgate, Mrs J.H. Clutton, distributed prizes on Friday evening at the Town Hall.

The fish market, 17 June 1917. All that remains are a few skeleton walls and shapeless brick piers as a reminder of the event, known as the Dump Raid, which destroyed it. The market, which was used as an ammunition store, received a direct hit by an aerial torpedo, which created all this havoc.

The west pier of Ramsgate harbour was the scene of an unusual incident on Thursday 17 May 1920. Just before noon there appeared on the pier an undertaker's hearse, directed by Mr G. Blackburn of York Street, Broadstairs, from which a coffin was gently removed. With the help of a hand-operated mechanical crane it was carefully lowered into Mr T. Read's motor boat, *Moss Rose*, on which a specially constructed bier had been affixed. The deceased lady had been engaged to a young man, when eighteen years of age, who was in the merchant service. On his last trip home he was accidentally drowned when his ship was passing Goodwin Sands. This lady was true to him in death, hence her wish to be buried in this fashion.

With the coffin securely settled and the floral tributes attached, the mourners boarded and took their place in the two motor craft. The cortège proceeded to a point near Goodwin Sands between the wrecks of the *Mahratta* and *Piave*. After the rector of Broadstairs (Revd L.L. Edwards) had intoned the committal service, the coffin was tilted overboard and sank in 20 fathoms of water. The remains were those of Miss Clara de Burgh Lawson, of Apsley House, Broadstairs, who died on 22 May at the age of seventy. She was the third daughter of the late Sir Henry de Burgh Lawson, Baronet, of Gatherley Castle, Yorkshire.

The crew of HMTMS *Minuet*, at Ramsgate harbour, *c.* 1918. She was one of fourteen tugs of the 'dance class' of mine sweepers, who all had dance-related names. This one was built and launched by Messrs Day & Summers of Southampton in 1917. The TMS (tunnel minesweeper) refers to the fact that the propeller of these tugs was placed within a recess, or tunnel, within the lower hull to allow operations in particularly shallow waters. HMTMS *Minuet* had a displacement of 290 tons.

A general view of the Royal Harbour, *c.* 1900. It depicts a selection of vessels settled in the inner basin and in the background is the Clock House which is now the Maritime museum. To the right is the ice house of the Isle of Thanet Ice Co., behind which you would find the fish market.

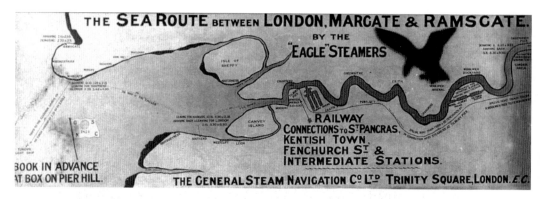

THE **SEA ROUTE** BETWEEN **LONDON, MARGATE & RAMSGATE.**
BY THE
"EAGLE" STEAMERS

RAILWAY
CONNECTIONS TO ST PANCRAS,
KENTISH TOWN,
FENCHURCH ST &
INTERMEDIATE STATIONS.

BOOK IN ADVANCE
AT BOX ON PIER HILL.

THE GENERAL STEAM NAVIGATION CO LTD TRINITY SQUARE, LONDON. E.C.

This intriguing map card depicts the sea route between London and Ramsgate taken by the Eagle steamers. The Eagle, one of the General Steam Navigation Co.'s early vessels, was the first steamboat to round the North Foreland to Ramsgate.

Above: A grand view of the town as the paddle steamer *Golden Eagle* enters the Royal Harbour at Ramsgate, *c.* 1924. The panoramic view is quite thrilling. The cost of these excursions varied: a saloon was five shillings, a fore cabin four shillings, children under twelve 2s 6d, and those in arms went free. Perambulators and bicycles were taken on board free of charge, at an owner's risk. The company's vessels left London Bridge Wharf for Margate and Ramsgate daily at 11.00 a.m., calling at Blackwell Pier and arriving at Ramsgate at 2.15 p.m.

Opposite above: Here is the complement of officers and ratings of HMS *Marshal Ney*, taken at Ramsgate, 1918. She was a monitor of 6,670 tons and was stationed opposite the entrance to the harbour mouth. Her armaments consisted of two 15-inch, eight 4-inch, and two 12-pounder guns, some of which can be seen here.

Steam trawler R19 *Provider, c.* 1933. Its owner was Mr Stanley Rowden and the vessel was built at S. Appledore in 1907. After 1923, there were only twenty-six smacks registered in Ramsgate. The days of the sailing vessels were coming to an end and steam trawlers had already begun to replace them.

This photograph is a poignant reminder of the price that some fishermen pay in their everyday business. The steam trawler, *Garrigill*, while on her journey to Lundy Island in August 1934, encountered a terrible storm which swept the Bristol Channel. Sadly, she was lost with all her eight hands. The men who perished in the disaster were: skipper Daniel Mynheer, mate Thomas Knight, chief engineer Ernest Bickford, second engineer Albert John Pointer, third hand Archibald Agutter, cook Robert Pedder, and deckhands Arthur Beavis and Thomas Cowell.

Ramsgate Sands, Friday 23 September, 1881. A favourite location for missionary Billy Knot was in front of the railway station on the Sands, where he carried out his religious teachings. This particular meeting was especially for the children and one cannot but admire the exuberance of this group, young and old alike. The photograph is by H.D. Hogben of King Street.

Built and engineered in Paisley, Scotland by Fleming and Furgusion in 1901, this is the Ramsgate dredger, *Hope*. It was owned by the Board of Trade and was later to be transferred to the Ramsgate Corporation from the 1 October 1934. It was subsequently sold to a Richard George Odell, who used to live on the Royal Esplanade, Westbrook, and was eventually broken up in October 1961.

The *Michael and Lily Davis* lifeboat. Watson Class arrived at Ramsgate on Saturday 21 November 1953 but it was not until Friday 11 June 1954 that the christening ceremony took place. The lifeboat was named *Michael and Lily Davis* by HRH the Duchess of Gloucester and after the ceremony a commemorative 150th anniversary vellum was presented to the Ramsgate lifeboat station. Pictured alongside the lifeboat is a high-speed lifeboat named *Dory*, which served on station from 1969-72.

HMS *Harrier* is a majestic sight as she enters Ramsgate harbour. When in port, the men of the Royal Navy were always ready to take part in social and sporting activities. This vessel is believed to be a minesweeper built by Thornycroft and completed on 17 April 1934. She ended her service in 1950.

The date of this visit to Ramsgate harbour by *H51 Scout*, a destroyer launched 27 April 1918, is unknown. Built by the Clydebank Engineering and Shipbuilding Co., Glasgow, Scotland, she was based at Hong Kong along with her sister ships the *Tenedos*, *Thanet*, and *Thracian*.

No seaside holiday was complete without a donkey ride on Ramsgate Sands, as pictured here, c. 1900. This view was sent to S. Debling of Ophir Villa with the message, 'I hope you are being kind to the donkeys'. Note the goat chaise on the left; ideal for tiny tots. There were two family-owned groups of donkeys on the Sands at the time, which often lead to disputes. These included one family taking another's customers and the drivers ending up fighting. The problem was finally settled by court proceedings.

DONKEY RIDES AT RAMSGATE.

This is a wonderful sight at Ramsgate Sands, c. 1950, seldom seen today on the beaches. All these smiling and happy children are having the time of their lives riding these friendly animals who had names such as: Snowy, PG 49, Jock, Sambo, Tony, Bonzo, Blackbess, Tom and Jeb. Could the man on the left be Aaron Todd?

An early photograph, *c.* 1880, of this popular area at the Sands railway station. The London, Chatham and Dover railway terminus did an excellent job of delivering many thousands of holidaymakers to the town and beaches. Sadly this area is now vacant after a disastrous fire and there is some fear over the new buildings and the effects they may have on the town and seafront.

This view of the Sands, *c.* 1890, was taken from an old photograph and what is remarkable is that all of the people are fully clothed – quite a contrast to today's ideology. The young boys in the foreground appear to be more interested in the cameraman than enjoying the sun, sand and sea.

An austere-looking building, this is Ramsgate Olympia's and the surrounding Merrie England, c. 1931. Lacking its final decoration, it replaced the Sands railway station. The new entertainments were liberally designed to accommodate the holiday tourists and local residents alike. The grand opening occurred during the month of June 1931.

Merrie England and the Olympia hall, now well established to receive one and all. The grand opening of the Olympia hall was held on Saturday 6 June 1935. Entertainment included dancing, sports and a mammoth gala held from 15th-20th July of that same year. This building was one of the largest amusement halls on the south coast and catered for thousands of visitors in wet and fine weather. During the Second World War, it served as HMS Fervent, a contraband control centre, and was decommissioned on Friday 14 September 1945 and returned to peacetime use.

Granville Marina esplanade experiencing bleak, stormy weather, Monday 29 November 1897.
Note the pier is withstanding the onslaught, but, as one would expect, the Marina Restaurant and
Theatre of Varieties, whose proprietor was F.C. Drew, is closed for the winter season!

East Cliff Bathing Station and Pleasure Sands, June 1914. This photograph, by A.H. Siminson of
Ramsgate, gives a good impression of the popularity of this particular area; indeed, it is possible to
note the slightly more relaxed attitude of some of the people on the beach. Note in the bottom
left-hand corner of the view the small refreshment kiosk. Soon their bubble of happiness was to be
dispelled by the declaration of war with Germany, on the 4 August 1914.

four

Entertainers

Marina pier, 1907. For this year's season, the lessees of the promenade pier, F.C. Dew and L. Valeriani, had secured the services of this popular group, the Zingari concert party, who gave free recitals throughout the season at 11.00 a.m. and 7.30 p.m. These concerts would be followed by dancing and more music. The charge for admission onto the Marina pier would be the princely sum of 2d.

This fine body of men – the Territorial Force – are staging their final tableau at the Royal Palace Theatre on the Wednesday night of 10 March 1909. They were all volunteers and were administered by the county associations. They were intended primarily for home defence purposes. This lighter side of their activities would compensate them for the normal rigors of their specialist training. Note the emblem in the centre of the group – Britannia with trident. This photograph is by M. Short, of High Street, Ramsgate.

The Salvation Army Drum and Fife Band. The combination of drum and fife was very suitable for the type of martial music required. The band gave their first musical festival at the Citadel on the evening of Thursday 21 November 1907. Donations were collected during the evening and the proceeds given in aid of the musical instrument fund.

The White Stars concert party opened their season in the Marina gardens on the evening of Saturday 7 June 1924. Frequent changes in programmes and attractive competitions were announced. The company included: Billy Peters, a comedian with plenty of 'go'; Gladys Carlton, a soubrette of charm; Alf Hicks, a light comedian and dancer; Alice Burns, Scotland's premier comedienne; Will Ingham, pianist entertainer and Arther Hines, lyrical baritone. All were fine artists who were welcomed once again by many local admirers and holidaymakers.

ST PRIZE

WINNER OF DANCING

COMPETITION

RAMSGATE. 1925

Left: This happy little girl at Ramsgate Sands, 1925, is showing off her talent. She is Dixie Ward, aged four, and is the winner of the first prize in this dancing competition. Many such competitions were held on the Sands to the great delight of the assembled audience who awaited some spectacle or dramatic entertainment. This photograph is by Reflex Snaps, of Granville Marina.

Below: Hosting the Holiday Express show at the Royal Victoria Pavilion, 1960. Billy Grant and Elsie Dunn, two fine dancers who thrilled the audience with their expertise and skill, were well into their dance routine. This type of variety entertainment is not really seen today, whether on stage or television.

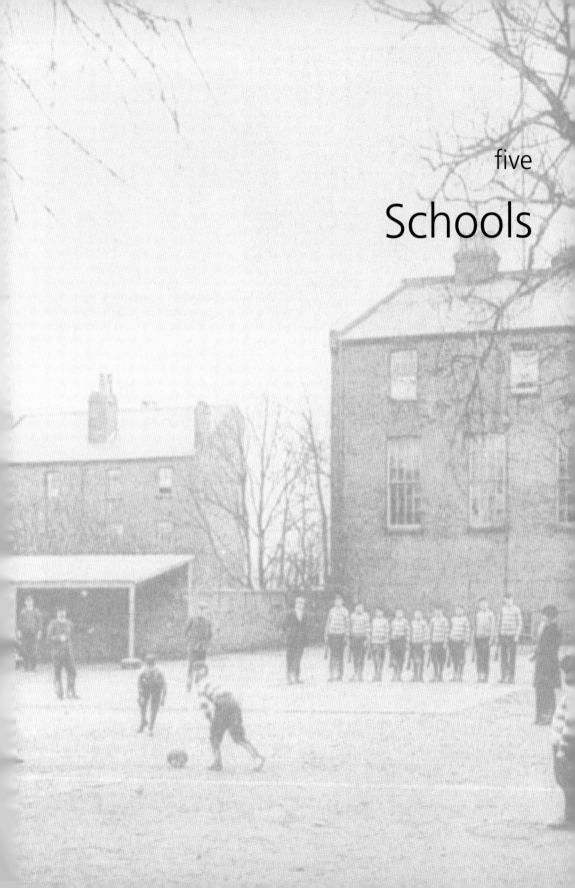

five

Schools

Bon Secours nursing home, London Road, *c.* 1949. This building was formally called Belmont and Westcliff House and was built by Joseph Ruse, *c.* 1795. A few years later it was purchased by Lord Darnley and in 1804 the property was purchased by Thomas Ware, remaining in his family until 1820. Queen Victoria as a child stayed here between 1828 and 1835. Another owner was Charles Murray Smith from 1904-22, who permitted annual fire brigade competitions to be held in the grounds. For a short period of time the premises were used as a hotel and called St Lawrence Cliff's Hotel.

This is a rear view of Bon Secours nursing home. From 1922, up until to the First World War, the building had a new use and became St Winifred's boarding school for girls. In 1921 the Bon Secours sisters took residence in a small house in Hereson Road called Victory Villas, where they ran a day nursery. This was later followed by a move to a house called St Benets in Spencer Square but for the duration of the war they lived in London. In 1948 the property was procured and renamed Bon Secours Nursing Home. Today it is called Westcliff Park.

Depicted here is the front and side elevation of Westcliffe school, Mount Edgecumbe, St Mildred's Road, 1903. The school was established on 15 August 1864. The aim was to provide the sons of gentlemen with an education to maintain their honourable positions in the world. Fees were inclusive, and were 50 and 60 guineas. Prior to this period of time there was public concern about the reliability of the local fire brigade since the terrible conflagration at Rose Hill. The owner of the school, Mr A.P. Southee, made sure his school building was prepared for any fire emergency. The building had two staircases as a means of escape fitted with internal fire hoses. It had fire extinguishers on each floor plus a supply of grenades, which were glass bottles filled with water – a very simple device and very reassuring for parents and pupils alike.

This view of Westcliffe school, taken in 1903, shows the rear of the building and sports field. Here we can see a portion of the extensive grounds which covered an area of 3 acres, where football was one of the favourite sports played. In the upper school the pupils, all boys, had a choice of two courses of study: modern was for boys wishing to adapt to a sea-faring life; and classical was for those wishing to enter university or the professions.

Left: There were many private colleges and schools in Ramsgate during the early 1900s, such as the Sloan Duployan Shorthand college, shown here on a greetings card from 1908. Its premises were to be found at No. 73, High Street, next to the Freemason's tavern. At the college, a rapid business and secretarial training in shorthand proficiency could be acquired, if you were an able student, in twelve weeks. As can be seen from the card, it was quite a family business.

Below: St Luke's girls school, class two, *c.* 1900. From left to right, back row: -?-, V. Dennis, E. Leigh, E. Friend, E. Biggs, W. Miles, F. Dray. Second row: V. Bradley, K. Langworthy, E. Read, H. Belsey, F. Hunt, G. Rutherford. Third row: J. Eudens, M. Hall, W. Hubbell, N. Earle, A. Beer, D. Paramor, F. Sutton. Front row, E. Beerling, E. Morgan, M. Carr, D. Carr.

Here are the Hereson school evacuees, Sunday 3 June 1940. As remembered by George Matthews:

We left home early and assembled at the school, where we were each given a brown tie-on label, with our names and identification details, to be attached to our jackets. We also had our gas masks, in their cardboard boxes, hanging by a string around our necks, with just a few items of spare clothing in carrier bags. We walked from school to Ramsgate railway station where we began the long, hot journey to the little village of Gnosall, in Staffordshire. On arrival we walked to the village school where this photograph was taken. The worst part of the day was when we were 'picked out' by the people of the village, not knowing how we would get on with our new families. My younger brother Len and I were picked together but my sisters Betty and Joyce were left 'unpicked' and there were no more villagers to take them in. A German, who was the local vicar, saved the day for us. He took them in until they were finally housed on a farm.'

Ramsgate Evacuees 3rd June 1940

Some of the names from the above image of evacuees: 1. John Holness. 3. Mr May. 4. Jack Norris. 7. Peter Champs. 9. Miss Scard. 10. John Christian. 12. George Matthews. 14. Jefferies. 16. Albert Bligh. 18. George Suckling. 20. Victor Lemare. 21. Peter Bennet. 22. William Bert. 24. Miss McKade. 25. A. Lawrence. 26. J. Lemare. 27. Joyce Matthews. 28. G. Gisby. 31. Betty Matthews. 32. Frances Saunders. 33. Betty Williams. 34. Mr Low. 35. Jefferies. 38. Ann Ansel. 39. G. Williams. 40. Pat Williams. 41. H. Smitthers. 42. J. Anning. 43. Margrett Bennet. 44. J. Burton. 59. David Suckling. 60. Len Matthews. 61. L. Norris. 63. Les Norris. 70. Jim Adems. 77. S. Kirby. 78. R. Liddle.

Ellington School's 2nd XI football team, who were champions 1923/24. Unfortunately, as it is quite often found with this type of view, there is no record of the players' names to be found on the back of the photograph. The football in the centre of this view is the only source of information. I have managed to come up with one name and that is W. Swan of No. 25 Hillbrow Road, Ramsgate. The photograph is by Bennet & Son, of No. 29 Addington Street.

This photograph shows Thornton Road elementary school, *c.* 1925, which was on Central Road at the corner of Bolton Street. It is a classic sign of the times, with four classes squeezed into one large room, and compared with the modern facilities of today, there is quite some difference. The only known pupil here is Lily Trumpeter, third from the left, second from the back. Notice how orderly and well-behaved the children all look. One of the school's favourite annual events was an outing to Sturry Woods near Canterbury, where the children would pick large bundles of bluebells to take home to their parents.

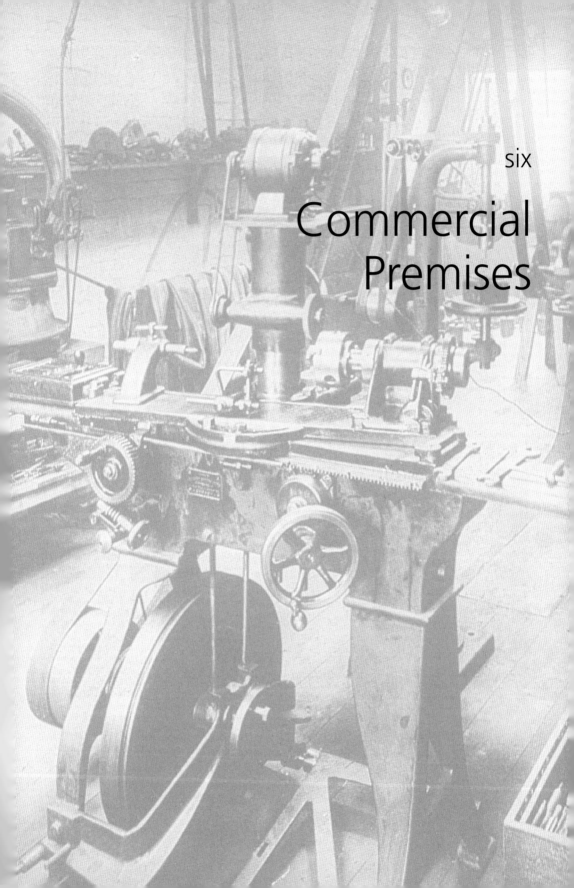

six

Commercial
Premises

WEIGHING, PACKING, AND MIXING FLOOR.

Above: This interior view of the mill of Hogben & Co., Thanet Mill, Margate Road, depicts the weighing, packing and mixing room ready for dispatching the produce to valued customers. Note the posters on the wall of Willson's Canadian Pig Powders. The photograph is by F.A. Thain of Ramsgate.

Ramsgate and District Electricity Co., Princes Road, *c.* 1905. It was not until the early 1900s that Ramsgate was to have its own electric-generating power station. But what actually went on behind the scenes in making electric power? The station was divided into four parts: the generation of steam, the generation of electricity, the intake of electricity and the distribution of it. Coal was brought from the Kent coalfields by rail and that fed the giant boilers in the boiler house which in turn provided steam to drive the turbines for the alternators. Also, later, in 1948, the intake of electricity came from the National Grid system and this was connected to two huge switches which fed the whole of the south-east section of Kent. The company offices were at No. 42 Queen Street; they bought the ground from the Ramsgate Corporation for £600. The cost of the building, which was erected by Mr J.W. Woodhall & Son of Ramsgate, amounted to £3,655. To the right of the view can be seen part of the premises belonging to Ellington Engineering Works.

Opposite below: Hudson's flour mill, *c.* 1967. Situated on the west side, or Margate Road, this familiar building dominates the landscape today. It was originally constructed in 1865 by Whitmore & Son, from Suffolk, and was named The Isle of Thanet Steam Flour Mill. It changed hands in 1891 and the new owners were the Hudson family. This mill was steam driven until 1937 when electric motors were installed. Further renovations took place in 1948 when a new plant was installed. Around 1969 the mill was operated by Rank, Hovis, and McDougall who were better known as R.H.M. Flour Mills Ltd. Sadly, the mill has closed its doors in September 2005 as it was found to be prohibitive to operate and the machinery was in need of major repairs.

Arthur Digerson Sackett, Church Hill, Monumental Mason, *c.* 1903. Besides producing new work the firm carried out renovation of old memorials and ecclesiastical subjects, but its speciality was in making memorials which were erected in any part of the country. The shop window displays an assortment of headstones but they also supplied tiled hearths, chimney pieces, and stone and marble mouldings.

The workshop of A.D. Sackett, Church Hill, *c.* 1903. The centrepiece of this view is the machinery used for cutting the stone and marble. In the bottom left-hand corner of the view can be seen an example of the workman's skill. The business of father and son served the community for seven decades before finally closing in 1965-66, and was replaced by K.R. Playford, joiners and paint manufacturers.

Right: Miss J. Holbourn proudly stands in the doorway of her shop at No. 155 High Street, Ramsgate, in the year 1931. This business was to be found on the corner of Eagle Hill and opposite the Eagle Hotel, and lasted approximately ten years. Today the building is still in existence.

Below: H. Bourne & Sons, which has been situated on the High Street since 1839. It occupied three large houses, listed as buildings, in the 1842 rate book. Mr Bourne next bought the newly built No. 33 in 1842 and No. 37 in 1872. Later, he acquired Nos 31 and 35 to become one of the largest drapers in the town. Note the splendour of the lamps and the heraldic insignia in between the first floor windows. This view was taken around 1890.

The High Street, Saturday 17 May 1915. The Bull and George Hotel was severely damaged after a zeppelin dropped twenty bombs on the town, which also damaged the fancy bazaar at Albion Hill and premises in Queen Street. As can be seen by the structure bridging the street, the hotel had to be fully demolished, eventually making way for the new Woolworths store.

Depicted here are the five survivors of the badly wrecked Bull and George Hotel. The location of the view and the names of the survivors are unknown. These are five very fortunate and lucky people.

VITTY & HOPPER,

Electrical Contractors, Fitters & Engineers.

Complete Electric Installations carried out in Town and Country Houses. Heating and Cooking Apparatus, Telephones, Electric Bells, Alarms, Medical Apparatus, Etc.

Head Office and Showrooms :

96, HIGH ST., RAMSGATE.

Telephone 41. Telegrams: "VITTY, RAMSGATE."

And at 14, King Street, MARGATE. Works: Chapel Place, RAMSGATE.
Telephone 57.

CONTRACTORS TO

H.M. Post Office. Ramsgate Corporation. Breadstairs U.D.C.
Isle of Thanet Tramway and Lighting Co.
Ramsgate and District Electric Supply Co., Etc., Etc.

Right: The head office and showroom of the electrical contractors, fitters and engineers of Vitty & Hopper, No. 96 High Street, Ramsgate, *c.* 1891.

Below: A.T. Fitchew's ironmongery and cycle shop at No. 75 High Street, *c.* 1898. Besides what is displayed in the shop windows, guns and ammunition were also on sale here as shooting was in fashion at this time. It was a popular sporting pastime when Thanet was surrounded by a more open countryside. Mr Fitchew also had his own workshops in Broad Street.

Stephen George Philpott, 16 High Street, c. 1885-99. He was a mineral-water manufacturer and confectioner who made the popular ginger beer brewed in 'ye old style'. Note the bottles lined up in the window and also the signs advertising the ale. His bottles in stone and glass are collectors' items today, especially those with the marble stopper type of glass bottle.

A truly remarkable scene in the High Street, c. 1904. Depicted on the left is the front of Sanger's Amphitheatre, as are the magnificent figurines and street lamps on the pavement. On the right side we have F.H. Welch, grocer, John Pain, stationer, Singer's Manufacturing Co. and John Perry, coal merchant. The High Street has been so named since 1790.

Fashion with Economy

ALL THE LEADING STYLES
IN SEASON'S GOODS
AT POPULAR PRICES.

GITTINGS & GITTINGS,

53, HIGH STREET,

RAMSGATE.

And at GILLINGHAM, CHATHAM.

Gitting & Gittings, No. 53 High Street. This is possibly a misprint, as this is the site of Herbert Frederick Welch, grocer. It later became The Westminster Bank Ltd and today it is known as NatWest Bank Plc. According to Kelly's *Directory of the Isle of Thanet*, Gitting & Gittings outfitters were to be found at 15 Queen Street on the corner of Cavendish Street from approximately 1925 to 1939.

W.H. Blackwell, confectioner, No. 11a and No. 13 High Street, *c*. 1925. Its location was very close to Turner Street. In the window of the shop on the right we can see a magnificent display of merchandise suitable for Christmas presents. On the left the display includes a variety of Cadbury's chocolates among many other items. Note the notice board in the centre of the view and the coffee and hot Bovril served with biscuits.

Left: This view of the High Street, from around 1897, has been produced from a glass negative and one cannot but admire it. The buildings are in pristine condition and the pony and trap trotting down the High Street is quite fascinating. Tom Wilson's Dining Rooms, previously called the Imperial Hotel, seem to dominate this corner of Chatham Street.

Below: T.W. Mockridge, No. 78 High Street, 1909. He was a master baker situated on the corner of Meeting Street. This very imposing shop, with the large advertising sign above the main door, was certainly bound to attract an enormous amount of attention.

From

T. W. Mockridge,

Pastrycook. Confectioner. Caterer. . .

Wedding Breakfasts.
Ball Suppers.
Receptions.
Dinners. ⊀⊀ Teas.

Catering for Large or Small Parties. Estimates Given.

John Kebble Chandler, grocer, of No. 117 High Street, *c.* 1925. This much-decorated shop window was arranged for a competition. The owners are looking very pleased with themselves and their efforts. Sadly, as stated on the back of this photograph, 'we never got a prize!'

Mrs M. Chandler, Fruiterer, of No. 131 High Street, *c.* 1931. She is standing in the entrance of her shop which was to be found on the north-east side of the High Street. She evidently did not like this photograph and requested the person she sent it to to destroy it. Fortunately, the person did not do her bidding!

Left: Lawrence Evans, fruiterer and general stores, of No. 68 Margate Road, *c.* 1931. This shop was situated next to A.E Turner, grocer and the Derby Arms public house, whose proprietor was Mrs E.J. Greig. Note the poster in the window, 'pure clean milk', supplied by H. Page & Son, Dairymen, of No. 20 Victoria Road. The lady in the forefront of this view is Mrs Esther Lawrence.

Below: These premises, Margate Road general stores, established in 1880, were on the corner of Kings Road and their proprietor was Mr Henry Collias. The property to the left is No.22 Margate Road and standing in the doorway is Mrs H. Collias senior. The shop window display has a wonderful selection of goods and is well worth a closer look.

Murphy Francis, Nos 30-32 Queen Street, 1905. This was a French boot and shoe depot and displayed in his shop windows is the autumn collection and winter stock. It specialised in boots at 14s 9d and 15s 6d, and also shoes at 8s 11d and 12s 9d!

Britton butcher's shop, Queen Street, c. 1897. This shop occupied the corner of York Street opposite Parkers the ironmongers. The selection of prime Scotch beef and prime Southdown lamb would inspire most people's appetites. The premises changed hands many times over the years, becoming: a florist, furniture makers, express cleaners, Oxfam and now, in the year 2005, Tea Pott's cafe.

Left: Ramsgate general hospital was opened 7 October 1909 by Lord Brassey, Lord Warden of the Cinque Ports. Two years earlier, on 24 November 1907, Capt. L. W. Vaile, president of the Ramsgate General Hospital, turned the first sod on the site of the new building. Today the site is called The Old Ramsgate Hospital and new apartments have been built on a portion of the grounds. The remainder of the surviving building is to be converted into twenty individually designed one- and two-bedroom apartments by Martin & Randle.

Below: Ramsgate general hospital, 1914. Private dwellings have now replaced the majority of these buildings. It is so sad to lose our heritage but modernisation and centralisation in this modern age will take its toll.

Harbour Parade, *c.* 1930. To make a living many men became self-employed and were very enterprising as hawkers. A certain section of the community tried to stop this type of street trading and restrictions were imposed as to what streets and roads they could use. This added to an unhappy situation for some years but eventually common sense prevailed. Here we see Edward Trumpeter displaying his attractively arranged produce on his barrow. Note that at the rear can be seen R.W. Tremain's tobacconist shop.

Keen's Dairy, No. 28 Bellevue Road, *c.* 1903. Depicted are employees of the dairy who are about to commence their work. Previously, the business was a lodging house but during the ensuing years there were quite a few changes of ownership. In 1913 it was owned by Robert William Forth, dairyman; in 1925, it was Stonelee's dairy; and just prior to 1931 the premises reverted back to a confectionery store whose proprietor was James William Benge.

K.D. Green, bookseller and stationer, of No. 5 Harbour Street, 1914. The previous owner was C.H. Willett, a bookseller and dealer whose ownership dated back to 1885, possibly even further. The window display has some very interesting articles including postcards appertaining to the military and royalty, a suitable theme at that moment of time. Ovendens, in 1925, eventually replaced Mr Green.

The Royal Paragon baths, *c.* 1891. With a commanding situation facing the western foreshore, these were erected in 1862 and were a state-of-the-art affair. Visitors could enjoy fresh seawater, ozone baths, and hot and cold water all the year round. With the passage of time its popularity declined and it was partly demolished with the intention of rebuilding, but such plans never materialized. It failed to survive the First World War.

Right: This photograph shows the shop and business of Charles James Fox, Chemist, of No. 35 Addington Street, handsomely decorated for the arrival and visit to the town by HRH Princess Louise. For his efforts Charles received first prize for the best decorated shop in town. To the right and adjoining the chemist's can be seen the family butcher's shop of William Shepherd.

Below: Situated on the corner of Bellevue Road, here are first-class fruiterers John and Thomas Turner, of No. 50 Plains of Waterloo, in 1903. A wonderful selection of vegetables is on display here but the item that catches the eye is the notice on the right, 'Blue Peas! Eight Pence a Peck'.

This postcard, of the Imperial Penny Bazaar, Albion Hill, established 1906, was sent to the Republic of Argentina on 23 July 1915. Note the fascinating selection of ornaments and dolls on display. The shop was twice wrecked by enemy bombardments, on 17 May 1915 and 17 June 1917.

William J. Stone, fruiterer, of No. 12 Grange Road, c. 1925. The firm's transport is lined up with laden produce ready for the day's delivery. They had a very good reputation for quick deliveries and their motto was: 'Quality the test for cheapness'. The shop to the left is Thomas Gilham & Son, furnisher, and the one to the right is Albert A. Latier, draper.

A composite and very decorative letter heading from the A & B Garage Ltd, Grange Road. The item itself is quite self-explanatory. Previous premises were at No. 4 Lorne Road, next to the licensed slaughterhouse at No. 19.

An impressive photograph of the A & B Garage Ltd on Grange Road, c. 1934. For the last thirty-two years this garage had been owned by Caffyn's motor dealership. With the demise of the MG Rover group, under which they had no control, they decided to close their business as of Wednesday 18 May 2005.

Corporation Gas and Water Offices
Ramsgate 7

Left: The Ramsgate Corporation gas and water offices, Boundary Road, were built in 1899. At the time of writing, the offices of this striking building are closed and vacant. Incidentally, the Gwen's clock in Queen Street has been restored and was unveiled by the town mayor, Steve Ward – could this building also be saved for future generations to admire? Above the main entrance is a very fine armorial insignia, well worth looking at.

Below: This photograph, by F.H. Treweeks of Queen Street, is of St Mildred's Hotel, West Cliff, *c.* 1936. This building has a chequered history. With the decline of the holiday trade a new venture was entered into and it was to become a guest house for the blind under the control of the Kent County Association. It was renamed Ogden House and became a residential home with forty bedrooms. Sadly, there was a decline in it use and it was finally sold at auction in February 1996.

Right: Matson & Co., dyers and cleaners, of No. 9 York Street, 1910. This postcard was sent to Miss E. Dale of Brighton, Sussex. It has an amusing comment on the reverse side, 'none of us like it here, we all think it mouldy, they took it one dinner time so of course the door was closed, it looks as if we are half asleep'. The shop is also the agent for R. Grant & Co., coal and coke merchants.

Below: Herbert's, confectioners and refreshment contractors, Nos 22 and 24 Harbour Street, *c.* 1900. The premises were previously, in 1898, Bryant & Co., bakers. In the 1920s they were occupied by the well-known chemist Boots (southern) who eventually took over No. 20 Harbour Street, which at one time was Richardson's Hotel, whose proprietor was Charles Holyer.

An advertisement for Perry's Coal, No. 66 High Street. The elegant centrepiece depicting *Old Goody* is in keeping with this establishment, which imported coal by boat.

Henry Thomas Pointer is proudly posing in front of his horse and coal wagon at No. 9 Brunswick Street, *c.* 1925. With a little imagination one can just see him meandering around the streets of Ramsgate selling his one- and two-hundred weight bags of coal, not an uncommon site from the past to dwell on.

This photograph features the premises of W.W. Martin, builders, at Dane Park Road, which were established in 1877. The occasion, names and date of this large gathering are unknown to me and I would be very pleased to gain further information. The firm is still well-organized in the area and is a mainstay for employment in and around Ramsgate. This photograph was produced by E.R. Morris.

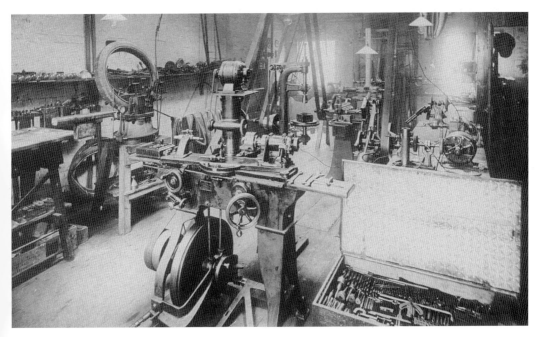

This interior view of Rayner & Co., motor engineering works, at No. 12 Alpha Road, c. 1931, depicts a well-established workshop. Other outlets of the company were at Cambrian Cottages and at No. 3 Townley Parade, Chatham Street, which had a cycle dealership. A previous owner of the garage in 1925 was Wilfred Andrews.

Portrayed here is the delivery cycle of the Butcher brothers' family business at No. 61 King Street, around 1929. Surveying the contents of the basket, it seems that a large order is about to be delivered, probably to a hotel or some other commercial premises. This era has long passed us by and today you would only see a trade cycle similar to this in a museum. By 1913 the business passed to William R. Lees and from 1936-39 to George Coleman.

Interior of the Northwood Mission church, October 1927. A chapel of ease to St Luke's church situated on the east side of Margate Road close to Pyson's Road. The pews are well-maintained and for the musical accomplishment there is the organ, depicted to the right in the view. The church, known as the Tin Hut, was brought from Brighton in 1884.

R.R. Rowland, confectioner, Harbour Street, 1946. Older generations may remember scenes like this. In this instance people are lining up for essential rations, sweets or sticks of rock. Following the Second World War it would take a decade before life returned to normal. Incidentally, this is where the late Ken Terry used to work.

The photograph depicts the interior view of Cave Austen & Co. Ltd, High Street in 1954, which for nearly half a century was one of the most popular venues for wedding receptions such as the photograph depicts. Many of the people here are well-established Ramsgatonians, including Goldsmiths & Deblings. To local people this business was always known as Cave's Café and as you passed the shop front a wonderful aromatic fragrance of roasted coffee beans attracted your attention.

Interior of Sharp's Dairy, Grange Road. Miss Betty Price is engrossed with the never ending task of preparing a continuous supply of milk for the populous. She worked for Sharp's Dairies Ltd, which later became Unigate Ltd, for twenty years and finally retired in 1974. A Ramsgatonian, Betty attended St Luke's and Ellington schools. During the Second World War she served in the RAF for four years with the very interesting job of Barrage Balloon Command, in which she excelled. She was a dedicated member of the Ramsgate Society but sadly she died during the summer of 2005. She will be greatly missed by many of her acquaintances.

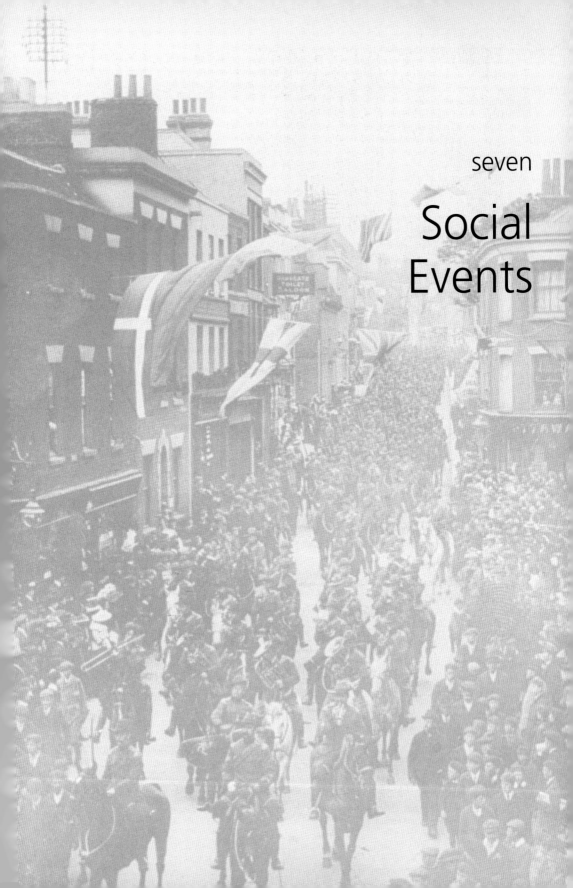

seven

Social
Events

Left: High Street, 20 May 1905. Not since 1867 has Ramsgate been honoured with a lengthened visit by the Royal East Kent Mounted Yeomanry. Back then they camped on the Ellington Estate. Today their camping ground will be at the grounds of the Murray-Smith estate, Pegwell. The town welcomed the Yeomanry in a 'right royal' fashion, with crowds of people and plenty of decorations. The Yeomanry finally met the mayor and corporation of Ramsgate before arriving at Pegwell to settle into their fortnight of intensive training.

Below: Tuesday 1 August 1905. General Booth is standing up in his white motor car as he approaches the pavilion. The mayor waited to formally welcome the grand old salvationist and his staff on behalf of the town and to congratulate him on his safe return from the magnificent campaign in the colonies. He had also campaigned throughout Scotland and England and this was eventually terminated at Chelmsford on 3 September. This was followed by a journey to London to attend a monster meeting at the Royal Albert Hall.

Thursday 18 May 1905. Mr Will Crooks, the well-known Labour MP for Woolwich, is seen here stopping outside of Travancore, South Eastern Road, for a few moments to have this fine photograph taken. With him in the vehicle are the Revd J. Gondie and Mr Richman, and all were involved with the Temperance and Evangelical Free Church council. Mr W. Crooks MP is in the lead vehicle of a large procession which traversed the town and started from the pier yard. Anyone interested could join in.

Chatham Street, 1906. This smartly turned-out parade of soldiers are a group of volunteers from Canterbury, Dover, Ramsgate and Sandwich about to depart for their annual camp. One of the Sandwich contingent was S.G. Cook of Vicarage Lane, Sandwich, who states on the back of this postcard that, 'this was taken specially for me'. On the right in the view can be seen the shop of Kirkaldie & Verrion, fishmongers.

Thursday 13 September 1906. The Battle of Flowers and Floral Fête, held in Ellington park, attracted an audience of 5,538 people and was a pleasurable event. There were many classes of subject to choose from, including motors, private carriages, trade vehicles, cycles and children's mail carts. Depicted above is one such section, all highly decorated with lovely flowers and a spectacle of beauty and brilliance. There was dancing for the children and concerts were given by the ex-British Guard and Royal Marine bands.

Saturday 8 June 1907. Depicted here is a passive resisters' demonstration at the return of the Revd B. Portnell from prison. The reverend gentleman had been taken to prison on the previous Monday for non-payment of the education rate and he was the first passive resistor from the Isle of Thanet to suffer incarceration for disobeying what non-conformists believed to be an unjust law. A large crowd at Ramsgate Town station awaited his homecoming and a procession was formed and headed by the Primitive Methodist church band, which marched through the High Street, Queen Street and Effingham Street to the Congregational Hall.

The visit of French mayors, Thursday 5 September 1907. Ramsgate had reason to be proud of the success of its reception of the French mayors, who were guests of the town for two days. There was a large and representative gathering at the Town Hall to welcome the guests. The band of the 7th Royal Fusiliers were in attendance. The market place can be seen in the above view, picturesque with its Venetian masts, floral devices and bunting. After the reception the French visitors drove through the principal streets of the town to the park where they witnessed the Battle of the Flowers. In the evening there was a banquet at the Granville Hotel. On Friday the visitors had a drive around Thanet and on return to Ramsgate the official visit was concluded, although many of the visitors stayed until Saturday.

Inauguration of the Territorial Force, Sunday 5 April 1908. The local units held a combined church parade and the Mayor of Ramsgate, Cllr J.H. Clutton, along with many other dignitaries too numerous to list, was in attendance. The band of A company, 4th Battalion – The Buffs – headed the units who marched from the artillery drill hall to St George's church. At the conclusion of the service the units marched via the High Street and Harbour Street to the pier yard, where General Sir Charles Warren presented two long service medals to Sgt Maj. Berry and Bombardier Coomer of the Old Artillery Volunteers. Sir Charles made reference to the patriotic spirit of the volunteers. The photograph is by T. Smith.

Left: The façade of these cottages is covered with a cluster of political posters prior to the election for a member of Parliament for Thanet, 1910. Unfortunately or fortunately, depending on whatever side of the political spectrum you were on, the results were: Mr Norman Craig (Con.) polled 6,892 votes compared to Mr Weigalls (Lib.) who polled 3,410 votes respectively.

Below: Police sports day, Ramsgate, 1910, which was open to all police forces in Kent, Surrey, Sussex and the metropolitan district. The most exciting event in this competition was the tug of war challenge. Here we have the Ramsgate borough police team overcoming their opponents from the West Malling division of the Kent county constabulary. During the afternoon the band of the Royal Marines and the Bijon orchestra rendered an enjoyable selection of music. In the evening the grounds were illuminated with fairy lamps. The mayoress presented prizes to the successful competitors on Thursday 4 August.

Empire Day, Friday 23 May 1913. Approximately 4,800 children, in their Sunday best, from nine elementary schools in Ramsgate, assembled in Ellington Park in celebration of this special day. The mayoress, Miss Gwyn, raised the Union Jack on the park flagstaff surrounded by the children in a semi-circle. The Ramsgate military band rendered various selections of music during the day. After the various events had concluded the children, on leaving the park, were presented with a specially made bun.

There was a large amount of interest in 1913 from various sports clubs in the town who organised walks to raise money for the local hospital. The distance of the walks varied but went up to six-and-a-half miles, and to encourage competitors valuable prizes were to be won. This event was, it is believed, organised by the Conservative Working Men's Club. Unfortunately, number six was not the winner. The location of this view is St Luke's Avenue.

Above: The Royal Sailors' Rest, on Harbour Parade. The tablet situated on the wall behind this group of people was unveiled on Thursday 6 May 1915 by the High Commissioner for the Dominion of New Zealand, the Right Hon. Thomas MacKenzie JP, MP. The society's Port Lyttleton branch of New Zealand had given a cot for wounded soldiers in the homeland and to commemorate this, this Royal Sailors' Rest was given to the Kent 2nd Voluntary Aid Detachment in the presence of Mr A. Lionel Johnson and Mrs A. Grummant.

Right: On Tuesday 8 May 1906 the Ramsgate Operatic and Dramatic Society performed the *Mikado* on the stage of the Assembly Rooms in the High Street. The gentleman depicted here is Bert and the comment written on the reverse of this postcard states that, 'when he moves his head, that thing comes right out and touches his feet!' This postcard was sent to a Miss Gifford of Clapton Common, London.

Below: York Street, 1914-18. Under a clause in the Aliens Bill, police in Ramsgate arrested several enemies in the town including a number of spies. They were placed in cells prior to being removed as prisoners of war and here they can be seen about to start their journey to Dover to be interned as such. The charabanc is a very early Albion. There is an interesting line-up behind the charabanc including a donkey cart, a handcart belonging to Mr H. Wells and a horse van.

Opposite below: The event depicted here is the bazaar which was held in a meadow of Mr Darby's farm, Northwood, on the afternoon of Thursday 12 August 1915 at 3.00 p.m. The mayoress, Mrs Dunn, kindly consented to open the bazaar with the support of other influential ladies and gentlemen. The object, with the generous help of Mr Ernest Perry and his wife, who was honorary secretary of the bazaar committee, was to raise funds for the external repairs of the church at Northwood. The net proceeds of this event amounted to approximately £25.

The Comrades of the First World War, December 1920. The aftermath of war was wrought with many difficulties, one of which was finding employment for all the personnel who returned to civilian life. The plight of these ex-servicemen, who walked the streets hungry when all they wanted was employment, was pitiful. Sadly, the local council was not a great help. The Comrades attempted to help themselves by making a house-to-house collection, asking for food, clothing and money but met with very little success. What was collected was distributed to those in need and each individual was given half a pound of margarine, bread, tea and sugar. The destitution in the town was sad to see and is a far cry from today's handouts from the appropriate authorities. Note the poster on the right-hand side in the view.

All ready for the annual charity match between Channel Company Chatham Reserves and the opposing navy team, Blue Jackets, in the grounds of Chatham House on Christmas morning, 1919. Admission to this event was 2d. The opposing navel team came from HMS *Hibernia* and *Juno* but the players' names are unknown.

Panther Patrol, 5th Ramsgate Troop, January 1922. From left to right, back row: ? Marchant, patrol leader; C. Silver; A. Bound; and ? Smith. Front row: L. Hodgman; ? Ward; and L Mills. Absent from this photograph is A. Hewitt.

This photograph, of the 2nd Ramsgate Girl Guides' Company along with the 2nd Ramsgate Brownie Pack, was taken in the grounds of St Luke's vicarage. The names of the girls and the date are unknown. One cannot but admire the smartness and pride felt by this group at that moment in time.

Ramsgate hospital, 1926. After HRH the Prince of Wales inspected the interior of the hospital, he is seen here about to meet the crew of the Ramsgate lifeboat *Prudential*. Included in this inspection were the three survivors of the crew who went to the wreck of the *Indian Chief* in January 1881. The men were Charles Verrion, eighty-two, David Berry, eighty-two, and H. Belsey, eighty-three. The Prince shook hands with each of the men and said he was delighted to meet such seasoned heroes. The vicar to the left of the Prince is the Revd J.M. Askwith, vicar of Christ Church and Chaplain of Ramsgate General Hospital.

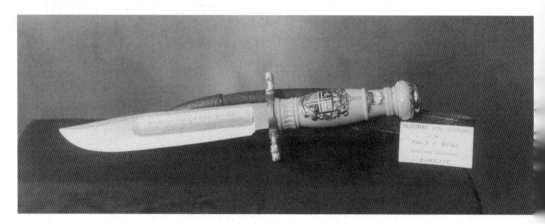

Depicted here is the presentation knife with which HRH the Prince of Wales cut the ribbons of the new promenade. It was a beautiful piece of Cutlers and Goldsmiths art and was in the form of a hunting knife. Twelve inches in length, the hilt was of carved ivory with silver gilt mountings and on one side, in enamel, can be seen the borough Arms. The blade, which was of polished steel, bore the following etched inscription: 'Presented to HRH the Prince of Wales, KG, KT, by the mayor and the burgesses of the borough of Ramsgate, on the occasion of his opening the West Cliff promenade and Under Cliff at Ramsgate, on 24 November 1926. F.C. Llewellyn (mayor), A. Blasdale Clarke (town clerk)'.

Ramsgate General and Seaman's hospital, 1926. The matron was Miss Alice Edgar, MBE. Here can be seen nurses and military personnel awaiting the inspection by HRH the Prince of Wales, as he progressed through his itinerary.

Nursing annual competition winners, 1925. This trophy was awarded to the three young ladies depicted in this photograph. Their leader was Miss Reeves and the other two were Misses Medland and Benham. The inscription on the cup reads, 'Presented by Lady Ambulance Officer Mrs Dunbar, after the annual competition amongst members of the Ramsgate Nursing Division, January 1925'.

Left: The Marina pool, East Cliff, Ramsgate. People on holiday and local people alike always enjoyed the facilities of this venue for pleasure and excitement. For children, the entrance fee was less than a shilling, with enough left over to buy an ice cream or drink By the smiles on the faces of these would-be beauty queens on the slide, it seems that they are certainly enjoying their visit to the pool.

Below: An aerial view of our most missed amenity, the Marina swimming pool, situated at the foot of the eastern cliffs with the sea lapping its outer perimeter. It is a landmark now sadly lost forever. Above the cliff the panoramic view includes the San Clu Hotel, now renamed the Comfort Inn and to the right are the Coastguard Cottages.

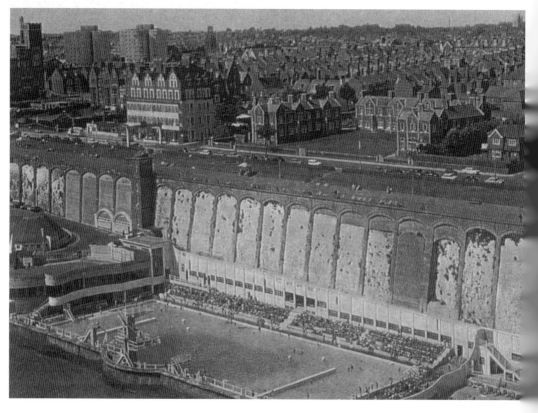

Right: Mercy Elizabeth Clara Hammon, aged five and of Ramsgate, is elegantly dressed for this special photograph. One cannot but admire this composition in its entirety. The pushchair and doll are in the proud possession of Mercy. Note the style of dress and the high leather boots.

Below: Personnel of County Steam Laundry Ltd, Grange Road, are enjoying their well-earned annual party, *c.* 1936. The majority of their names are unknown but perhaps someone may recognise their grandparents or parents within this photograph.

Left: The County Rink, Dumpton Park Drive, Saturday 27 April 1912. Depicted above is Mr Ernest May the floor manager, along with Dolly Grant, skating instructor and Professor Batch. All three are splendidly dressed in the costumes appropriate for the evening's entertainment which was a grand fancy dress carnival.

Below: The new County Rink opened on Saturday 30 July 1910. Flags decorated the interior of this one-time factory which was splendidly adapted for roller skating. Hundreds of residents and visitors attended the opening ceremony but no local dignitaries were present. Mr A.G. Shoolbred, the chairman of the board of directors, stated that, 'it would be best to ask the public to perform the opening ceremony themselves'.

COUNTY RINK
RAMSGATE

Right: La Belle, Alliance Square, *c.* 1936. Mr H.C. Hunter, landlord of the Camden Arms Inn, proudly displays his magnificent collection of prizes for his chosen sport – fishing. The top right-hand trophy is inscribed with 'The Royal Ramsgate Fishing Club'.

Below: St George's Old Boys' football team, 1957-58, who won the Kent Junior Cup. The final match took place at Brett's sports field, Canterbury, on Good Friday, 4 April 1958, where they triumphed over Thannington with a final result of 3-2. The players' names are unknown except for the scorers, who were: D. Evans (2) and D. Bellingham (1).

A Christmas visit to the North Goodwin lightship, Wednesday 30 December 1953. For the first time that year lightship men at North Goodwin received a visit from the Mayor of Ramsgate. In this picture, Cllr E.G. Butcher expresses the town's greetings to the men on the job at Christmas. The visit to the lightship was an annual one made by the local chaplains of the mission to seaman. The Reverends are T.G. Leech and J. Eric Blanchett. In coxswain Doug Kirkaldie's motor boat, *Salvor*, the party took with them Christmas fare, books and other gifts given by the townspeople for the men on board the lightship.

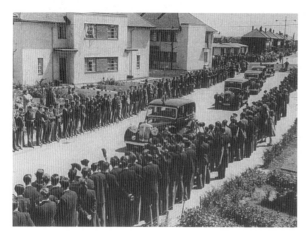

Crowds of people thronged Durban Avenue on Thursday 1 June 1950 to see HRH Princess Margaret, on her first visit to Ramsgate, as she was about to carry out her duties. First, she named the principal thoroughfare of the Newington estate, formally Durban Avenue, after herself. Later, she planted a tree at the estate's centre and finally cut the first sod on the site of the 1000th council house.

Here we see, at Ramsgate carnival in 1950, local members of the Kent Civil Defence Force taking part in the carnival's festivities. The ladies, Mrs M. Philpot and Cecilia Brooks, are giving their best and trying to entice the spectators to part with their money. All proceeds went to local charities.

Ramsgate carnival, 1954. Depicted in the foreground is the popular float supplied by Tomson & Wotton, the local brewers. This is followed by the Dumpton Greyhound Stadium entry. Unfortunately, no prizes were won at this event and today, sadly, we have only mementos of these two businesses left, but the memories linger on.

Jacky Baker's sports field, the venue for the Easter hockey festival, 1952. Beryl May Forde, second from the right, is having a welcome break between games, surrounded by her colleagues. Approximately fourteen pitches were in use and during the four days of the festival 150 games took place, with 700 players competing. This was Ramsgate's fifteenth hockey festival.

Beryl May Forde, the co-founder of the Ramsgate Ladies' Easter Hockey Festival, at Jacky Baker's sports field, c. 1955. Beryl was born in Ramsgate and lived in the town for ninety years before moving to Nottinghamshire. She was a keen sportswoman, playing tennis and hockey. Here she is seen entering Jacky Baker's sports ground via Highfield Road, ready for action.

eight

Transport

Left: Granville Marina, *c.* 1927. The motorbike and sidecar was a very popular mode of transport then as it is today. Here, a happy family of five are making the most of the restricted space available. Obviously, today this would not be permitted for safety reasons. In the background can be seen the front of the Marina Dance Hall where jollifications materialised every evening, commencing at 7.00 p.m. Catering was available for all the family.

Below: The sign is for everyone to see, informing them that a motorcycle gymkhana, to be held at Southwood football ground, was to be staged by enthusiastic members of the Invicta Motorcycle Club. The event took place on Saturday 30 July and Monday 1 August 1938. All parties were warmly welcomed to this attractive annual open air event and all monies collected were donated to local charities.

Friday 27 March 1908. A long and well-organised procession representing the brewers, distilling and allied trades, parades to and from the Royal Victoria Pavilion to demonstrate against the government's new Licensing Bill. The procession, which took place in the afternoon, attracted much attention and a special meeting was held at the Royal Victoria Pavilion, which was packed. Various speakers, including the parliamentary member for Thanet, were most enthusiastically received.

The motor mail service between London and Ramsgate commenced on Wednesday 1 July 1908. Depicted here is the vehicle in all its glory: a Milnes-Daimler lorry converted into a mail van. The location of this view is unknown but it could be A.D. Hodgman's livery stables behind King Street.

The weather was ideal on Tuesday 19 August 1913 when Mrs W.H. Oliffe of the Bellevue Hotel accompanied the well-known airman Monsieur Salmet as a passenger in this frail-looking *Daily Mail* monoplane. The flight was over Ramsgate and it lasted eleven minutes, encompassing Ramsgate and Broadstairs. After the flight Mrs Oliffe said that, 'the town looked like a toy from the air and it was such a lovely sensation that I want to do it again'.

F.R. McLean leaving Ramsgate
Aug 1st 1914   W.J. Miller

Mr McLean, the owner of this private seaplane, arrived in Ramsgate on Wednesday 29 July 1914. The following afternoon an excited young man, master Jack Weigall, was privileged with a flight. Depicted in this view is Mr McLean taking off on Saturday 1 August, The background of the landing stage enhances this view. The photograph is by W.J. Miller.

The Lord of the Manor corner, Sunday 2 July 1922. This marked the junction of the Ramsgate, Canterbury, Margate and Sandwich crossroads where many motor accidents have taken place, and it was, on this Sunday afternoon, the focus of a terrible collision between two powerful touring cars, both laden with passengers. Unfortunately, the smash ended fatally for two ladies travelling in one of the vehicles, with more or less serious injuries occurring to four other people. Miraculously enough, although no fewer than fourteen persons were riding in the cars, eight escaped with nothing worse than shock and bruises.

Lord of the Manor corner. The vehicle depicted is the one on the right in the top view and is a 7-seat, 20hp Austin owned by Mr Charles Samuel Farris of South Bermondsey. Prior to the accident there were seven people in this vehicle. Two ladies, Mrs Sherrin and Mrs Chapman, lost their lives. The Ramsgate Fire Brigade, who converted the fire engine into a temporary ambulance and conveyed several of the injured to the local hospital, carried out valuable work. Their prompt services gained them a special vote of thanks from the town council.

Albion Hill, Friday 2 May 1924. Mr Newton David Munro Turvey of No. 194 St James Court, London, left his car, a four-seater touring model Daimler, standing unattended outside No. 3 Albion Place for a few minutes. Suddenly, for some unknown reason, the car started to run down the incline towards Harbour Street, crashing into the balustrade and hurling some 30ft of masonry onto Madeira Walk some 20ft below. The car ended up in a most perilous position, with the near front wheel hanging over the edge of the rockery. Eventually the car was attached to a charabanc, which was backed down the hill, and was towed to safety. Thankfully no one was injured. The sequel to this affair, at Ramsgate police court on Monday 19 May, was a fine of £5!

This City of Canterbury registered vehicle, belonging to the East Kent Road Car Co. Ltd, remains a mystery. It was supposedly part of an incident which took place in the Ebbsfleet or Stonar area.

nine

Public Houses

The Bellevue Inn, *c.* 1925. The proprietor was William Henry Olliffe. It was an attractive building with an elegantly positioned lamp with etched- and stained-glass inserts, and was once a landmark on the corner of Bellevue Road and Plains of Waterloo. There have been questionable press accounts over the ownership and location of this beautiful lamp, but it is believed that they've been resolved. Time will surely disclose the answer. Note the lady and child standing on the veranda – Mrs Olliffe, perhaps?

A general view of Harbour Parade, *c.* 1898. This is a copy of an earlier photograph reproduced by local photographers Carr & Son, in 1936. All of these buildings were demolished to make way for improved vehicle access, through road widening, to the Sands railway terminal.

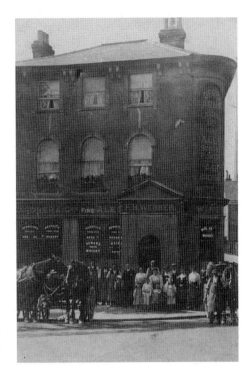

The Derby Arms, Margate Road, on the corner of Princes Road, 1909. This family group photograph was especially taken for a relative who lived in Essex. It was sent to Mr James Serby reminding him that these were all of his relatives living in Ramsgate. I wonder if that included the draymen? As can be seen, this was a Gardner & Co. Ltd house, whose beverages were supplied by the Ash Brewery.

Interior view of the Derby Arms, Margate Road. Looking very serious are Madge and Alex, two more of Mr Serby's relations, who do not include the creature standing on the bar! An attraction to the many customers who frequented this house, Its real purpose is unknown?

A very homely and friendly establishment, this is the Admiral Napier, of York Terrace, pictured in 1905. The managers were Mr John Hilyer and his son, who are standing here in the doorway. Note the two placards attached to the iron railings, one advertising sea trips on the *New Moss Rose* and the other a visit to London on the *Southern Belle*.

Admiral Napier, York Terrace. This is a later view depicting a wider range of buildings but the Admiral Napier distinguishes itself by the advertising appendages on the side of the building. On either side of this Tomson & Wotton public house can be seen boarding houses and tearooms which have sadly now all passed into history.

The York Arms, Nos 33-35 King Street, *c.* 1936. As the sign boldly shows, this is a Truman's house. Although not very large, it was a well looked-after establishment under the management of George Albert Squire. In the bottom left-hand corner of the picture can be seen Mrs Squire. To the right can be seen a notice in the window stating: 'No Drinking Outside'.

The Hare and Hounds Inn, *c.* 1925. Its landlord was Thomas Lawrence. Situated on the edge of the borough boundary, on the Margate Road, this inn was in an ideal position to cater for travellers along this route. One of many Tomson & Wotton houses, it is still flourishing today.

The Flying Horse public house, of No. 50 Park Road and adjacent to Ellington Park, *c.* 1903. The brewery supplying this establishment was George Beer of Canterbury. During 1931, the tenant landlords were Mrs M.A.E. Clayson and Miss F. Gibbs, and from 1936-39 it was Mr Harry Barnes Sutton.

The Brown Jug, 1903. This idyllic scene depicts the halfway house bordering between Ramsgate and Broadstairs. The area still retains its village atmosphere and the innkeeper, James Saunders, is standing in the doorway. Cobb & Co., the Margate brewery established in 1673, supplied this house.

Charles Holyer was tenant and landlord of The Harp public house, of Nos 108-10 Harbour Parade, seen here in 1913. This was another Tomson & Wotton house but with a difference, because if you look to the left you will see The Harp Music Hall, reputedly one of the earliest music halls in the country, dating back to 1876. Above the establishment can be seen Kent Terrace and a glimpse of Albion House.

The Wheatsheaf Inn, High Street, St Lawrence, *c.* 1936. Its tenant landlord was Joseph Henry Wood. The group of people immediately in front of the inn are about to board their charabanc; they include, on the far left, Mrs S.A. Porritt, *née* Silvester, who was at one time a local councillor and Justice of the Peace. After a considerable number of years' service to the community, she retired from the bench on 31 December 1971.

The Duke of York, No. 22 Addington Street, c. 1925. During the Napoleonic wars this building served as a canteen for the troops stationed in this area. It was only after the hostilities ceased and the troops moved away that it was converted, in the early 1800s, into a public house. The landlord of this establishment during this year was Thomas John Johnson.

The Windmill Inn, 1951. Situated on Newington Road at the corner of Whitehall Road and built in approximately 1930, the inn is little changed today. As we can see, this was another Tomson & Wotton house but when the brewery closed there were many changes in and around the town with suppliers, giving customers a larger choice of beverages, much to the delight of most people.

ten

Out of Town

Cliff's End hall, 1 September 1912. Reputedly said to be over 400 years old, this was once little more than a cottage, enlarged in 1876. Early in the twentieth century Miss Derry, of the celebrated Kensington store Derry & Toms, owned the hall, which included a large wooded area that was opened to the public on certain occasions. Sadly, in recent years the hall was demolished and many of the trees were to be removed to make way for a modern housing estate 1973-78.

This truly rural scene is of Little Cliff's End farm, c. 1925. The building is situated off Chalk Lane and is overlooking Pegwell Bay. Sadly, the thatched barn has been allowed to fall into a derelict condition but the animals seem to be well cared for. If you were inclined to walk along the footpath from Pegwell, you may be pleasantly surprised by what you see.

Right: Saturday evening, 15 August 1953. More than half a century has passed since this event happened. Following in the footsteps of St Augustine, 200 territorial troops of the 10th Parachute Battalion, belonging to the County of London Regiment, dropped on a pre-arranged landing zone in Pegwell Bay before forming up to commence their weekend exercise. This is a photograph of the only known local lad who was involved. Note the large amount of equipment carried and only one parachute! It is needless to say that the exercise to capture the American-occupied Manston aerodrome was a success.

Below: Pegwell Bay, 15 August 1953. Large crowds of holidaymakers were at this spot to witness an unusual event. About to unfold before their eyes was a giant weekend exercise involving thousands of territorial troops. The scene over Pegwell Bay on Saturday evening depicted one of five troop carrier planes belonging to the American 12th Troop Carrier Squadron, which was based in Germany, dispatching paratroopers over the dropping zone at the commencement of the exercise.

A view of the old Tudor house at Pink's Corner, Way, Minster. This house is reminiscent of the characteristics and style of the Tudor period 1485-1603, with exposed beams as a typical feature. It was not important enough to be restored and sadly It is not known when it was demolished. Since its demolition, other buildings have been erected on this site.

A tranquil view of Monkton Road looking west, c. 1936. The exact date is not known but very little has changed in this area today. As can be seen, it is still a very peaceful and tranquil village road. Note the absence of motor vehicles.

Ebbsfleet House, to be found just outside the western boundary of Ramsgate. It was in this area that the historical landing of Hengist and Horsa, and later of Augustine with his forty monks, followed by many a shipload of marauding Danes, took place. Since these early days the sea has receded and between Ebbsfleet and the present beach there is a mile's breadth of reclaimed land.

Monkton, c. 1925. As its name implies, this was originally a village of monks and during William the Conqueror's time it had its own fisheries and salt works. Depicted in this view is the Wesleyan Chapel. To the left of the chapel is Vulcan Villa where a Miss Hales lived.

The New Inn, Monkton, *c.* 1903. The proprietor was a Mr Frederick Hodgman and here he can be seen with his family posing for the camera in front of his premises. The Chic Photo Co. of Margate produced this postcard.

Monkton Village, *c.* 1904. The parish of Monkton is two miles north-west of Minster Station and six-and-a-half miles west of Ramsgate. The population in 1901 was 409. This early postcard depicts a picturesque village thoroughfare. Note the group of boys in the centre of the view who probably attended the National school which was erected in 1870. The average attendance was eighty children and the master was Mr W.H. Burgess.

Right: Monkton, 1947. For those who enjoy the countryside, this is a view to admire. I have travelled this road but maybe because of changes over the years I was unable to find this exact location. A young lady called Bertha sent this postcard to a Mrs Balmer in Surrey and she states that, 'This view is near to where I am staying, going to a little place this afternoon called Minnis Bay, near Birchington'.

Below: An aerial view of Walters Hall caravan and camping site, Monkton, *c.* 1955. This recreational activity is greatly pursued by those who like fresh air and freedom. Here, with the added attraction of the seaside and all it has to offer, it is not surprising that this is just one of many such sites in the area.

Other local titles published by Tempus

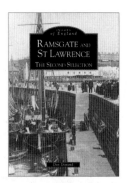

Ramsgate and St Lawrence: The Second Selection
DON DIMOND

This selection of over 200 photographs of old Ramsgate and St Lawrence range in date from the late nineteenth century to the advent of the hovercraft terminal in the late twentieth century. Ramsgate was described in 1891 as 'the queen of Kentish watering places', and this reputation as a haven for holidaymakers is illustrated here with images of crowded beaches, seaside entertainment, well-loved boarding houses and hotels.

0 7524 2460 2

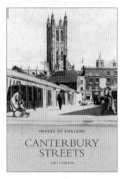

Canterbury Streets
JANET CAMERON

This book examines the streets of Canterbury in an attempt to detail the history of the people and places contained within them and create a sense of the past here. Discover the derivation of the old streets' names, how they have changed and the new routes in this many-layered city. Canterbury Streets will delight those who know the area as it was and those who live in the city today.

0 7524 3398 9

Haunted Kent
JANET CAMERON

Haunted Kent contains spooky stories from around the county, including the hunchbacked monk at Boughton Malherbe, the black dog of Leeds and the well-known tale of Lady Blanche of Rochester Castle. This fascinating collection of strange sightings and happenings in the county's streets, churches, public houses and country lanes is sure to appeal to anyone wanting to know why Kent is known as the most haunted county in England.

0 7524 3605 8

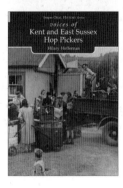

Voices of Kent and East Sussex Hop Pickers
HILARY HEFFERNAN

Right up to the late 1950s, the annual hop-picking season provided a welcome escape for thousands of families who lived and worked in the poorer parts of London, who would migrate every year to the hop gardens of Kent and Sussex to pick the harvest. The photographs and reminiscences in this book tell a fascinating story; of hardship, adventures, mishaps, misfortune and laughter experienced during hardworking holidays among the bines.

0 7524 3240 0

If you are interested in purchasing other books published by Tempus, or in case you have difficulty finding any Tempus books in your local bookshop, you can also place orders directly through our website

www.tempus-publishing.com